Space Walks

Space Walks

Robin Kerrod

GALLERY BOOKS
An Imprint of W. H. Smith Publishers Inc.
112 Madison Avenue
New York City 10016

Contents

Half Title Page: Astronaut Robert Stewart
tests the manned maneuvering unit on shuttle
mission 41-B.
Title Page: Gemini 4 Astronaut Edward White makes the first
American walk in space on 3 June 1965.
Contents: During the 41-B shuttle mission Bruce McCandless is
carried remote manipulation arm.

Credits
Most photographs in this book were kindly supplied
by NASA/Spacecharts. Additional photographs
were provided by the following,
to whom many thanks:
Robin Kerrod, pages 15, 37 and 68;
Novosti/SPL, page 11; Spar Aerospace, page 58.

This book was devised and produced by Multimedia Publications
(UK) Ltd.

Editor: Jeff Groman
Production: Arnon Orbach
Design: Michael Hodson
Picture Research: Susan Hormuth/*Picture Research,* Washington

First published in the United States of America 1985 by Gallery
Books, an imprint of W. H. Smith Publishers Inc., 112 Madison
Avenue, New York, NY 10016

ISBN 0 8317 7965 9

Origination by D S Colour International Ltd, London
Printed in Italy by Sagdos, Milan

Introduction

'Firing the thrusters of his 'Buck Rogers' style backpack, astronaut Joe Allen jets across to the gently rotating *Palapa* satellite. He docks with it using an ingenious piece of equipment, aptly named the stinger. With controlled bursts of the thrusters, he stops the satellite spinning and then jets back with it to the shuttle orbiter *Discovery*. There, he and fellow-astronaut Dale Gardner, with workaday efficiency, manhandle it into the payload bay and secure it.'

A few years ago this scenario could only have been imagined in a science fiction story. But today it is science fact. The drama of the Palapa satellite capture was enacted on 12 November 1984, some 220 miles (350 km) above the Earth at an Earth-relative speed of 17,500 mph (28,000 km/h). Two days later a near-identical capture took place of a Westar communications satellite.

Satellite capture, spacecraft inspection and repair, and in-orbit rescue, are just a few of the things that spacewalking astronauts can now accomplish. NASA's term for such out-of-this-world experiences is extra-vehicular activity, or EVA.

The first 'walker'

It is now over two decades since astronauts first dared to leave the protection of their spacecraft to brave the deadly environment of space. Russian cosmonaut Alexei Leonov blazed the spacewalk trail when he emerged briefly from his spacecraft Voshkod 2 on 18 March 1965. At that time, the Americans seemed to be in danger of losing what was becoming known as the 'space race' – the drive to become the pre-eminent nation in space. On the Mercury flights between 1961 and 1963, four American astronauts had logged a mere 34 orbits around the Earth. This compared with no fewer than 275 orbits logged by seven Russian cosmonauts. First woman in space, Valentina Tereshkova, alone had spend much longer in orbit than all the American astronauts put together! And now the Russians were seen to be pulling even further ahead in the race, with spacewalking.

Very soon, however, this was all to change as NASA's two-man Gemini Project got underway. The first manned Gemini mission went into orbit just a few days after Leonov's pioneering spacewalk. Then, in June 1965, the second Gemini mission soared into orbit for a near 100-hour flight. Most significantly on this mission, astronaut Edward White made a spectacular 21-minute spacewalk.

More spacewalks followed as the Gemini missions progressed towards a triumphant conclusion in November 1966. The objectives of the missions were to verify procedures that would have to be carried out during the next great leap forward in space exploration – the conquest of the Moon. They were all well and truly achieved.

The scene was now set for the Apollo Project and the landing of American astronauts on the Moon. By 1969 all the Apollo hardware and software had been thoroughly tested on Earth and in space. On 20 July Apollo 11 set down on the Moon, and Neil Armstrong planted the first human footprints in the lunar soil. He became the first of a unique breed of 'moonwalkers', whose spectacular excursions across the lunar surface mesmerized hundreds of millions of Earthbound TV viewers.

Spacewalking astronauts met and overcame yet another challenge at the beginning of the next major project: the Skylab space station in 1973. They successfully repaired damage sustained during the launching of the space station, which would otherwise have caused the cancellation of the project. Thanks to their ingenuity, the project thrived and led to the last team of Skylab astronauts smashing all previous space duration records. They remained aloft for 84 days, still the longest any Americans have spent in orbit.

Routine adventure

After Skylab, no American spacewalks took place until 1983, well into the shuttle era. But since then, spacewalking, like shuttling, has become routine. It is already making possible successful satellite recovery and repair operations, and in the years ahead will feature prominently in the construction of space stations and even more ambitious space structures.

Bruce McCandless passes yet another milestone in spacewalking history by floating untethered for the first time, on 7 February 1984. He is making the first test flight of the jet-propelled manned maneuvering unit. It works perfectly, making possible later in the year some spectacular satellite repair and recovery missions.

1 Suited for Space

Here on Earth we live cocooned by a layer of air we call the atmosphere. The atmosphere gives us oxygen to breathe. Without it, we would die. Although we are not generally aware of it, the atmosphere presses down on us with a pressure, at sea level, of 14.7 pounds per square inch (1 kg per square centimeter.) Our bodies are adapted to living at this pressure. If they are subjected to greatly increased or greatly reduced pressure, body functions, particularly breathing, are impaired, and life is put at risk.

The atmosphere also helps keep us warm. At night it acts like a blanket and helps prevent the daytime heat the Earth absorbs from the Sun from escaping into space. Too much cold will kill us. So, on the other hand, will too much heat. The atmosphere helps the Earth environment maintain a balanced temperature, which averages about 22°C.

Beware Radiation

The atmosphere has yet another function that ensures our survival. It acts as a filter and blocks out the dangerous radiations that come from outer space. These could otherwise make life very unpleasant and over a long period maybe even eliminate life as we know it.

One of the major hazards to life is the ultraviolet radiation given out by the Sun. Fortunately for us this is largely filtered out by a thick layer of ozone (a three-atom form of oxygen) about 30 miles (50 km) above the Earth. The ultraviolet rays that do get through are generally welcomed because they are responsible for our sun-tan! But those of us who have stayed too long in the Sun know how easily they can burn. Without the ozone layer, ultraviolet radiation would become a killer.

Another radiation hazard is posed by the streams of penetrating atomic particles that reach the Earth from space. We generally call them cosmic rays. They consist of charged particles such as protons, electrons and mesons. Other charged particles stream to the Earth from the Sun in the form of the so-called solar wind. Again the atmosphere helps block them, as it also does the Sun's X-rays and gamma-rays.

Particle radiation does not pose so immediate a threat as ultraviolet rays. But it is far more insidious. This is because the radiation can penetrate the body and damage the living cells. It can give rise to cancers and leukemia, a disease caused by the destruction of the red blood cells. In the longer term, the radiation can affect future generations because it can alter the sex genes which govern heredity, and cause possible mutations.

The Space Environment

From this long list of dangers, you can guess that if we attempt to leave the cocooned comfort of Earth's atmosphere, we become exposed to an extremely deadly environment. Even a fleeting exposure of an unprotected human body to space would result in a particularly unpleasant, but mercifully quick death.

Space is to all intents and purposes a vacuum. There is no breathable air or any other gas present to exert pressure. Freed from pressure, the blood and other bodily fluids would boil. We would experience unendurable agony as gas bubbles formed and tried to escape through the body tissues. Deep-sea divers who have undergone sudden decompression would know what to expect – a lethal attack of 'the bends'.

With no blanket of air to modify them, temperatures in space fluctuate wildly. In the Sun, temperatures soar to more than 150°C. In the shade they fall to below -100°C. Radiation is ever present. Also present in varying degrees are dust particles, generally called

Fully kitted out in spacesuits and backpacks, Apollo 16 astronauts Charles Duke (left) and John Young rehearse procedures they will follow when they touch down on the Moon. Behind them is a replica lunar rover, which they will use for transport over the lunar surface.

micrometeoroids. Larger particles storm through from time to time. These are the ones that cause the flashes of light that, when seen from Earth, are called meteors.

Life Support

So when human beings venture into space they must be comprehensively protected. They must take with them their own mini-atmosphere. They travel inside a pressurized spacecraft, in which a comfortable environment is maintained by a so-called life-support system. The crew-cabin has a double wall, which helps reduce the danger of depressurization in the event of a meteoroid hit.

The pressure maintained in early spacecraft tended to be on the low side. Apollo, for example, had a pressure of only about one-third atmosphere. And it was pure oxygen. Skylab also had a one-third atmosphere pressure, but used a mixture of oxygen and nitrogen. The space shuttle, however, uses a near normal Earth-type atmosphere of 80% nitrogen and 20% oxygen at ordinary atmospheric pressure.

Supplying pressurized oxygen is only one requirement of a life-support system. It must also regulate the temperature and humidity of the air to provide a comfortable 'shirt-sleeve' environment, essential for the working astronaut. In this respect it acts like an ordinary air-conditioning unit. Further features of the system include a fan to keep the air circulating, and a screen to catch floating debris, such as hair and crumbs.

Last but not least, the life-support system must have a 'scrubber' to remove the carbon dioxide the astronauts exhale. If the carbon dioxide level were allowed to build up, it would cause drowsiness and headaches and in large enough doses, suffocation. The scrubber removes the carbon dioxide by circulating the air through canisters of granular lithium hydroxide. The canisters also contain layers of charcoal, which remove odors from the air.

Spacesuits

The early astronauts, on the Mercury, Gemini and Apollo missions, flew into space in spacesuits. The present generation shuttle astronauts do not. They wear spacesuits only when they go spacewalking. The design of spacesuits has changed substantially over the years as the role of the astronaut has changed, from test pilot to moonwalker to do-it-yourself satellite repairer.

The Mercury spacesuit was not really a spacesuit in the modern sense. It was simply a pressure suit designed to serve as a back-up system in case the Mercury capsule accidentally depressurized. It was a modification of the standard US Navy high-altitude pressure suit. It consisted of just two layers: an inner pressure layer of rubberized fabric and an outer restraint layer of nylon to prevent the inner one 'ballooning' when it was inflated. The outside was aluminized as a heat-reflective coating (or, say some, to make the astronaut look more like the popular image of a spaceman!).

The Gemini astronauts were given an improved suit because it was intended that they should leave their spacecraft and go spacewalking. Their suits had extra layers to give them added protection from the space environment. For life-support they were connected by a tube, or umbilical, to their spacecraft's on-board life-support system.

Then came the development of the Apollo spacesuit, which proved the major breakthrough in suit design. It was designed as a multilayer garment that could be supplied with air via an umbilical or by a life-support backpack, or portable life-support system (PLSS). The various layers together provided all the necessary means of life support and protection not just for a short period, but for prolonged extravehicular activity.

The basic suit worn by the Apollo astronauts had three layers – an inner cloth comfort lining, a rubber-coated nylon bladder as the pressure layer, and then an outer nylon restraint layer to prevent ballooning. There were flexible joints at the body joints. The suit contained a system of cables and the equivalent of a block-and-tackle system that allowed the astronauts to move their arms and legs more

Right: Dr Kathryn Sullivan (left) becomes the first American woman spacewalker in October 1984, during shuttle mission 41-G. Here, she relaxes off-duty in orbit with Dr Sally Ride, who is making her second trip into space.

Top right: Cosmonaut Alexei Leonov blazed the spacewalk trail in March 1965 during a Voshkod mission. He is pictured here during the joint American-Russian mission, the Apollo-Soyuz Test Project (ASTP) in July 1975.

Main picture, right: Cosmonaut Svetlana Savitskaya becomes the first woman to go spacewalking in August 1984. She is pictured here working with equipment on the outside of the space station Salyut 7.

Below: The pioneering Apollo 11 astronauts, pictured before their epic journey to the Moon in July 1969. On 20 July Neil Armstrong (left) becomes the first Earthman to set foot on the alien world. Edwin Aldrin (right) joins him later, while Michael Collins remains in orbit.

easily. This had always been a problem when suits were pressurized.

Apollo astronauts embarking on EVA were more extensively equipped. Instead of the inner comfort lining next to the skin, they wore water-cooled combinations, or 'long johns'. These ensured a steady temperature no matter what the astronaut's physical exertions. Over the restraint layer of the basic suit came a 17-layer protective oversuit. The PLSS was a miniaturized version of the spacecraft's life-support system, having an oxygen supply, lithium hydroxide canister, and water-cooling system, batteries and radio and telemetry (communications) equipment. The complete Apollo EVA suit and accessories – PLSS, helmet, control box, gloves, boots and so on – weighed 190 pounds (86 kg). An Earth-bound astronaut would have found this unbearable. Thanks to the low gravity on the Moon, however, the astronauts only had to shoulder one-sixth of this weight.

Above: The original seven astronauts who took part in the Mercury program, which launched the first American into orbit. They are, from left to right: back row, Alan Shepard, Virgil Grissom and Gordon Cooper; front row, Walter Schirra, Donald Slayton, John Glenn and Scott Carpenter. Their silvery spacesuits are based on the pressure suits used by high-altitude pilots.

Above: Dr Sally Ride models the current shuttle flight suit, in which astronauts now travel into orbit. It is a far cry from those of yesteryear. Shuttle astronauts have no need for spacesuits since their craft is fully pressurized, like terrestrial airliners.

Right: Apollo 15 astronaut James Irwin gets kitted out prior to launch in July 1971. A technician is fitting one of his gloves, which is fixed and sealed by a snap and twist connection. The helmet is attached in a similar way. The Apollo crew always wore their spacesuits during the launch operations.

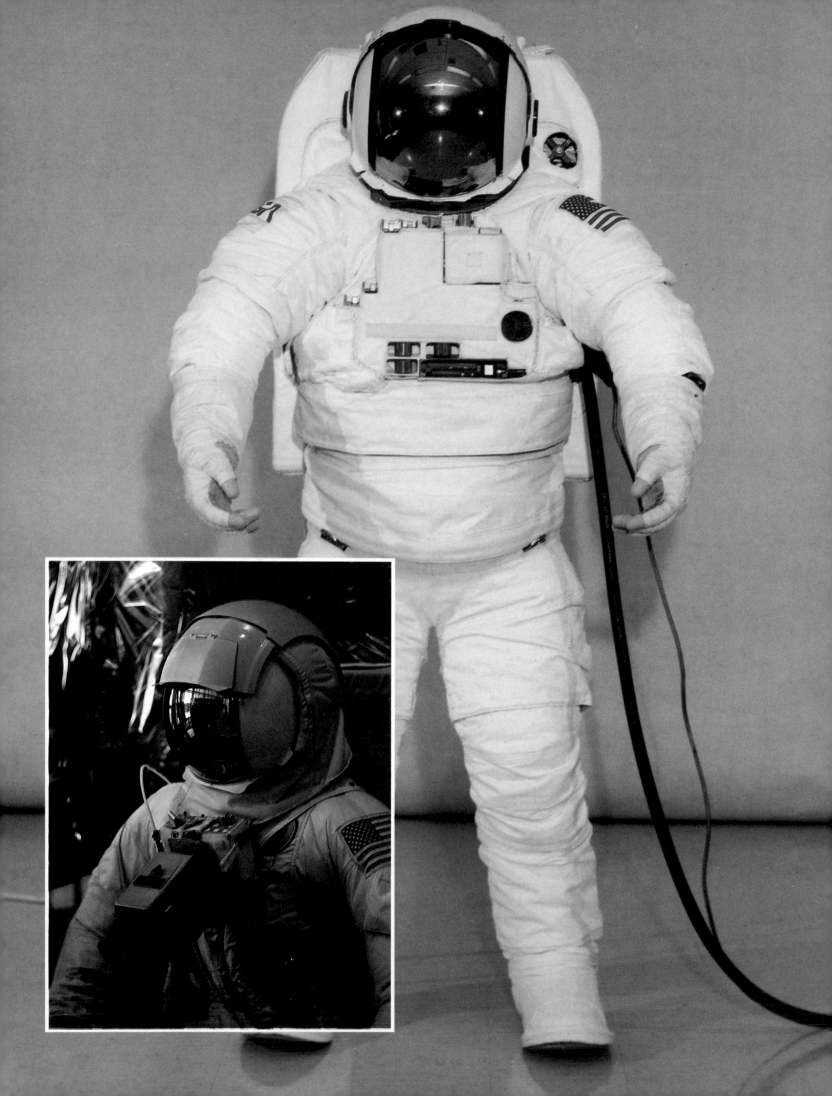

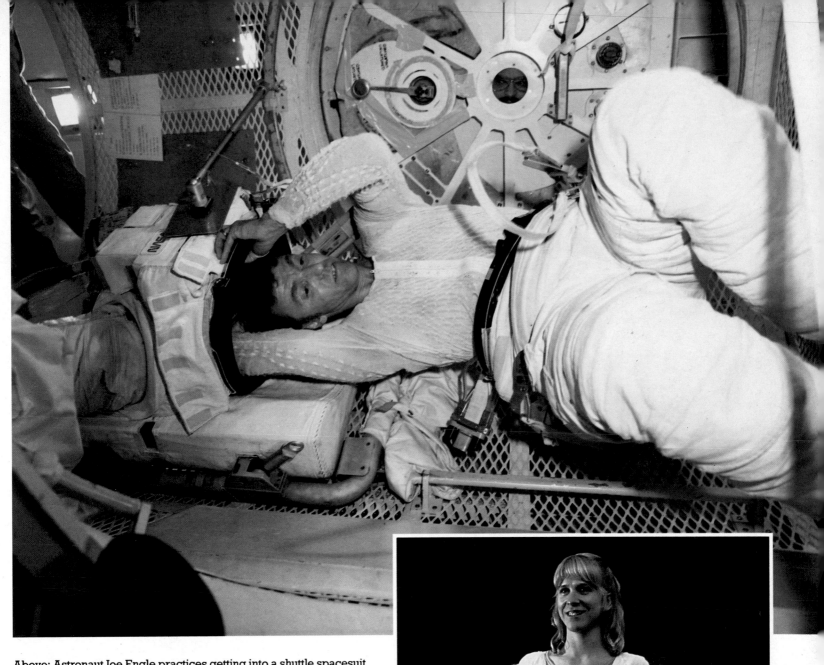

Above: Astronaut Joe Engle practices getting into a shuttle spacesuit during simulated zero-G conditions aboard an arcing aircraft. The technique is to don the trousers first and then float up into the torso. It is not as easy as it seems.

Left: The modern shuttle spacesuit, or EMU (extravehicular mobility unit), which is worn only when an astronaut exits the shuttle orbiter to go spacewalking. It is a two-piece suit consisting of a torso and trousers, which connect and seal at the waist. Life-support is provided by the backpack, which is integral with the torso.

Far left: An Apollo spacesuit for comparison. Note the external connections on the chest, a feature absent in the modern shuttle suit. But the helmet and visor assembly is much the same.

Right: The 'long johns' worn by shuttle astronauts beneath their spacesuit. The garment has tubes running through it, through which cooling water is circulated to keep the astronaut's body temperature steady. The tubes connect with a water supply in the torso backpack.

Right: Skylab astronauts practicing for EVA. They are immersed in a huge water tank called the neutral buoyancy simulator at the Marshall Space Flight Center at Huntsville, Alabama. As it turned out, the first crew of Skylab astronauts would need to do some unscheduled spacewalking to repair the damage suffered by the space station at launch.

Bottom: Neutral buoyancy training still forms an essential part of spacewalk preparation. Here Norman Thagard practices exiting from the shuttle orbiter airlock hatch into the payload bay. The hardware is a full-size mock-up of the orbiter, which is accommodated in the neutral buoyancy simulator at the Johnson Space Center at Houston, Texas.

Below: The test director at the neutral buoyancy facility at Houston. He takes the water-borne astronauts through the procedures they will eventually follow in space. According to the astronauts, anything they can do in the simulator, they can do more easily in space.

2 The Umbilical Era

Manned space flight for the United States began on 5 May 1961. It was a little over three weeks since the Russians had launched their first cosmonaut into space. He was Yuri Gagarin, who made one complete orbit around the Earth in a Vostok capsule on 12 April. He reported that he could work satisfactorily in the weightless conditions in orbit. He returned to Earth none the worse for the experience, after a flight lasting 108 minutes and over 25,000 miles (40,000 km). The breakthrough had been made. Until then, no-one knew for sure whether a human being could withstand the stresses of space flight: punishing acceleration at lift-off, weightlessness in orbit, and deceleration and frictional heating during re-entry into the Earth's atmosphere.

If for no other reason, national prestige demanded that an American should get into space as soon as possible. So on 5 May Alan Shepard climbed into a Mercury capsule, named *Freedom 7,* on top of a Redstone booster at Cape Canaveral, Florida. At a little after 9.30 a.m. local time, he was blasted off the launch pad for a suborbital flight; one that would take him out into space and then back, without going into orbit. It was a brief flight – 15 minutes – in which he was weightless for only about 5 minutes. All went smoothly and augured well for the future American space program. The Russians, however, were unimpressed. Premier Nikita Khrushchev called the flight 'a flea jump'.

Before Congress, twenty days later, President Kennedy announced that the United States had accepted the implied Russian challenge for supremacy in space, and urged that no effort be spared to land an American on the Moon before the decade was out. Incredibly, the United States was to achieve this aim, with five months to spare.

Into Orbit – At Last

As a further test of the Mercury capsule, astronaut Virgil Grissom, made another suborbital flight in July 1961. And then on 20 February 1962, John Glenn rose into orbit for the first time. He circled the Earth three times in his capsule, *Friendship 7.* Three more Mercury flights took place over the next 15 months, concluding with Gordon Cooper's 22-orbit mission in May 1963.

On the Mercury project the astronauts were little more than passengers. The capsule was cramped to say the least, and the astronauts could scarcely move a muscle. There was no question of them spacewalking. No-one really knew whether they could even survive in space inside a spacecraft, let alone out of it! On the proposed flights to the Moon, however, astronauts would be required to take a more active role. They would need to be able to maneuver their craft and rendezvous with other vehicles. They would need to stay in space for long periods and be able to work outside their spacecraft.

It was the object of the next phase of the American space program to achieve these goals. The project was called Gemini, meaning 'twins', an appropriate name for flights by the two-man spacecraft. The Gemini capsule itself gave the astronauts only slightly more room than the Mercury, but it was equipped with two large hatches over the astronauts, which they could open in orbit.

The Gemini EVAs

The first manned Gemini mission (Gemini 3) took off on 23 March 1965. Aboard were Virgil Grissom, later to perish in a fire during an Apollo training session, and John Young, who was destined to become commander of the space shuttle on its maiden flight 16 years later. The new spacecraft was put through its paces and passed with flying colors. In June of the same year, Gemini 4 blasted off with James McDivitt and Edward White aboard. Tragically, White would also die later in the Apollo fire that claimed Grissom's life.

Tumbling head over heels, Edward White makes his historic spacewalk in June 1965. The picture shows one disadvantage of the early EVA suit: the astronaut tends to become entangled with the umbilical supplying him with oxygen. The umbilical is also vulnerable to accidental damage.

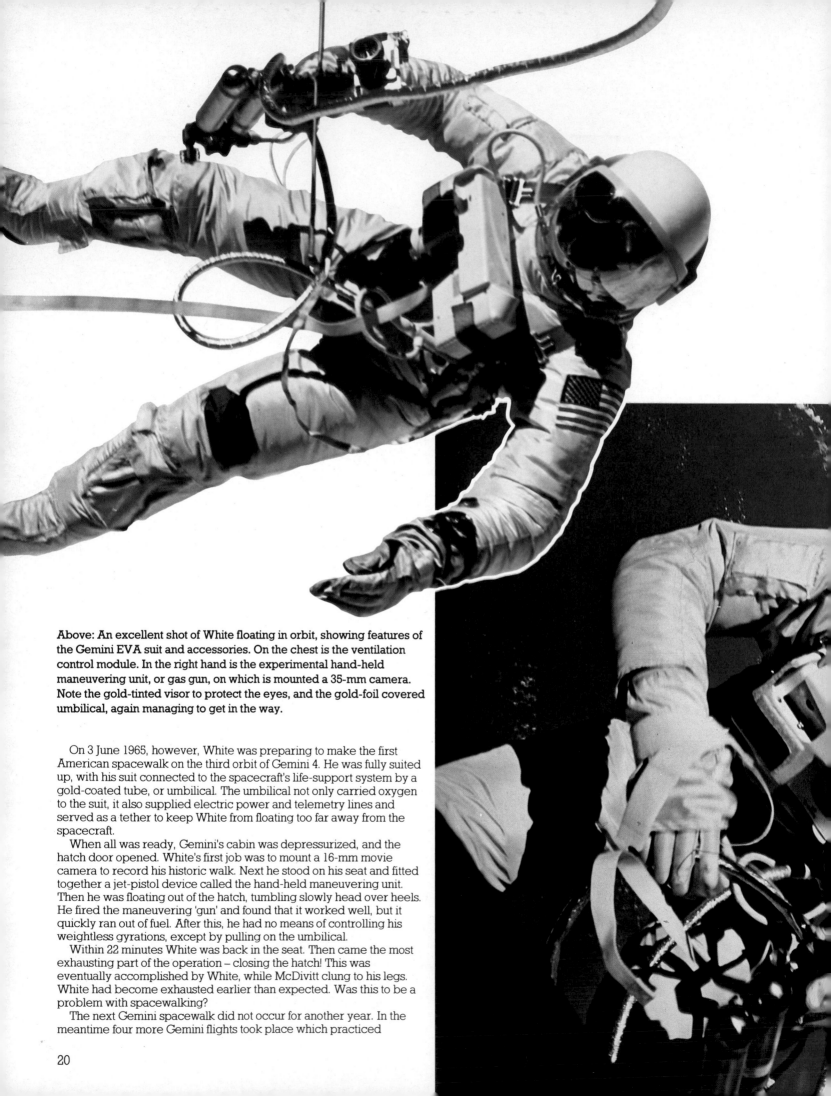

Above: An excellent shot of White floating in orbit, showing features of the Gemini EVA suit and accessories. On the chest is the ventilation control module. In the right hand is the experimental hand-held maneuvering unit, or gas gun, on which is mounted a 35-mm camera. Note the gold-tinted visor to protect the eyes, and the gold-foil covered umbilical, again managing to get in the way.

On 3 June 1965, however, White was preparing to make the first American spacewalk on the third orbit of Gemini 4. He was fully suited up, with his suit connected to the spacecraft's life-support system by a gold-coated tube, or umbilical. The umbilical not only carried oxygen to the suit, it also supplied electric power and telemetry lines and served as a tether to keep White from floating too far away from the spacecraft.

When all was ready, Gemini's cabin was depressurized, and the hatch door opened. White's first job was to mount a 16-mm movie camera to record his historic walk. Next he stood on his seat and fitted together a jet-pistol device called the hand-held maneuvering unit. Then he was floating out of the hatch, tumbling slowly head over heels. He fired the maneuvering 'gun' and found that it worked well, but it quickly ran out of fuel. After this, he had no means of controlling his weightless gyrations, except by pulling on the umbilical.

Within 22 minutes White was back in the seat. Then came the most exhausting part of the operation – closing the hatch! This was eventually accomplished by White, while McDivitt clung to his legs. White had become exhausted earlier than expected. Was this to be a problem with spacewalking?

The next Gemini spacewalk did not occur for another year. In the meantime four more Gemini flights took place which practiced

Above: The first American spacecraft to be designed for EVA, the two-man Gemini. This picture shows the Gemini 7 capsule in orbit some 160 miles (260 km) high. It is taken from Gemini 6 on 15 December 1965 during successful orbital rendezvous maneuvers.

Left: Pioneering spacewalker Edward White emerges from the open hatch of the depressurized Gemini 4 spacecraft on 3 June 1965. He says the experience 'must be worth a million dollars!'. He spends more than 20 minutes outside.

rendezvousing and docking in orbit. Eugene Cernan began the second spacewalk from Gemini 9A in June 1966. It was intended to be much more ambitious than White's. It required Cernan to float to the rear of the spacecraft and put on an Astronaut Maneuvering Unit (AMU). This was a backpack containing life-support equipment and thruster units. Thus equipped, Cernan would then jet around the spacecraft, master of the space environment.

It was not to be, however. Cernan, like White before him, tired quickly as he struggled to unpack and slip into the AMU. The problem was that he couldn't keep still. It was the old action-reaction principle. If he tried to turn something one way, his body would also turn around by reaction. Cernan's temperature rose, his pulse rate soared to 180 beats per minute, and he began to sweat profusely so that his visor misted over. He had to abandon the task and end the EVA.

On the next Gemini mission (Gemini 10) Michael Collins was more successful. Using a nitrogen-powered hand-held maneuvering unit, he jetted over to an Agena target vehicle they had rendezvoused with and retrieved from it an experimental package designed to detect micrometeroids. On Gemini 11, Dick Gordon attached a tether

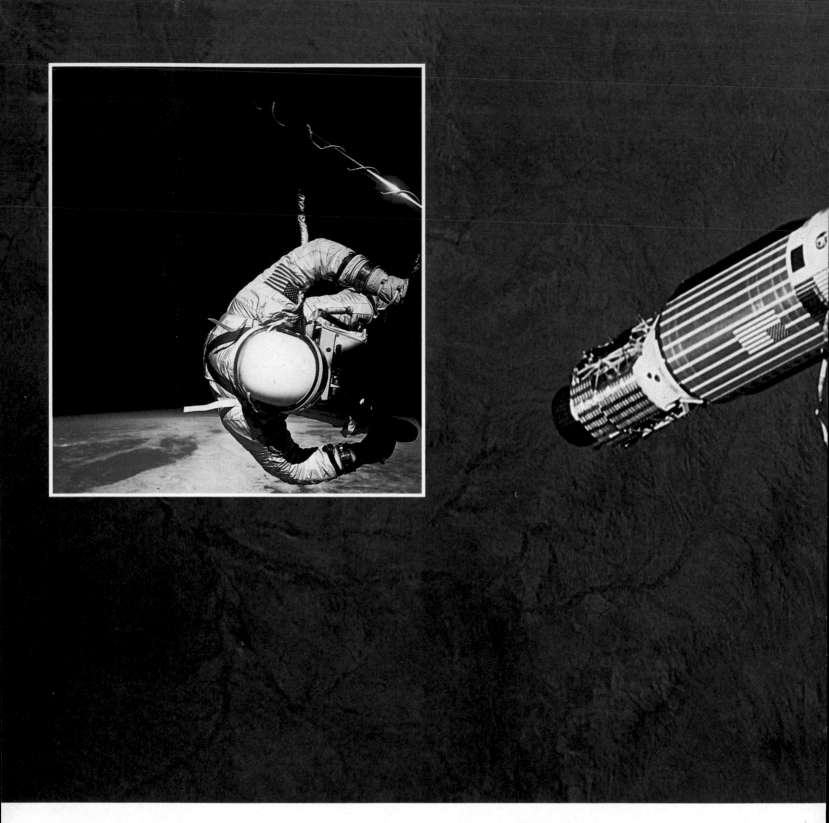

between an Agena target vehicle and the spacecraft. The tethered complex was then rotated, creating a trace of artificial gravity. Again Gordon became exhausted and his suit system couldn't cope with the increased temperature and moisture from his perspiration. On the final mission, Gemini 12, in November 1966, Edwin Aldrin's spacewalks were much more successful, and he was not so readily fatigued as his earlier colleagues. In three EVAs he was exposed to space for over 5½ hours. His next spacewalk was to be historic for, less than three years later, it would take place on the Moon.

Skylab

The Gemini project gave way to Apollo, and along with it came the much improved Apollo spacesuit. The suits were designed primarily for the lunar EVAs when the astronauts used backpacks (see Chapter 3). But they could also be used with umbilicals when necessary.

Some of the Apollo astronauts performed umbilical EVAs to change film packs when returning from the Moon. The Skylab astronauts also performed umbilical EVAs. The first team that visited Skylab really did wonders when they were sent up into orbit on 25 May 1973. Their job was to repair the space station that had been launched 11 days earlier. During launch, one of Skylab's solar panels and a micrometeroid shield had been ripped off. Another solar panel had not been properly deployed. The spacecraft was short of power and overheating.

But the astronauts quickly and ingeniously cured the trouble. Working through an access hatch from inside Skylab, they rigged up a thin metal 'parasol' over the damaged area and shielded it from the Sun's rays. The temperature inside soon began to fall. Later they went out through the Skylab airlock and succeeded in freeing the jammed solar panel. Skylab was now fully operational, and set for three missions that would break all existing space duration records and acquire invaluable data, particularly in space medicine and solar physics.

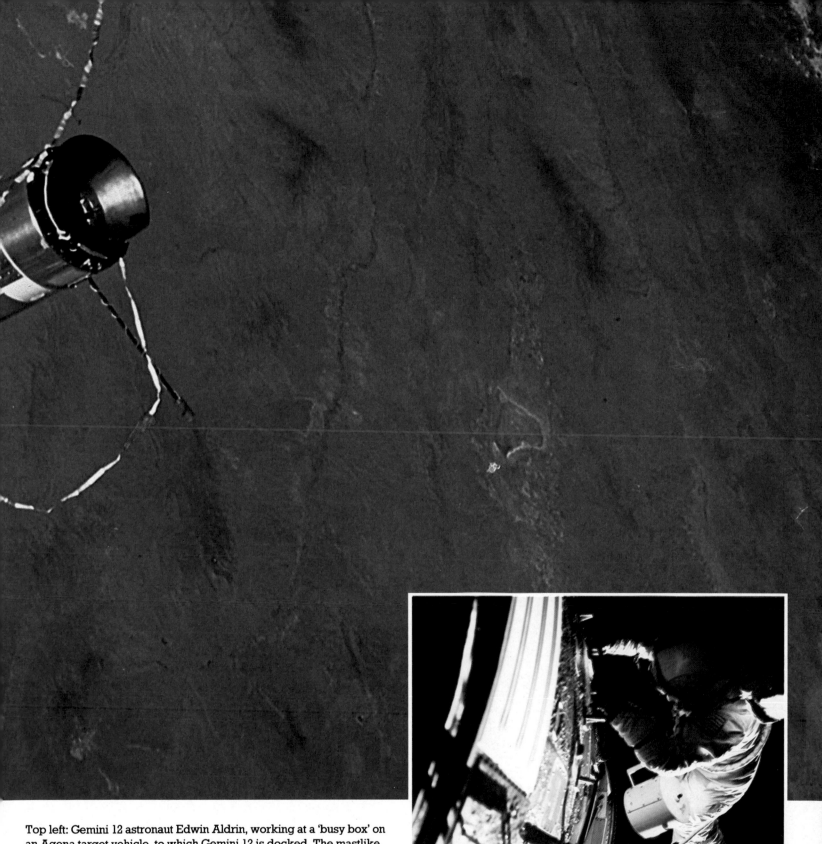

Top left: Gemini 12 astronaut Edwin Aldrin, working at a 'busy box' on an Agena target vehicle, to which Gemini 12 is docked. The mastlike antenna of the Agena can be seen in the picture. Aldrin's EVA, on 12 November 1966, proves to be the most successful of the Gemini missions. His next EVA will be historic – it will take place on the Moon.

Main picture: The Gemini 12 Agena target vehicle. At the end closest to the camera is the docking cone. Earlier the Gemini spacecraft was docked with it, and during this time Aldrin attached a tether between the two craft. Pilot Jim Lovell is now backing away from the Agena to get the tether taut. Then he will conduct artificial gravity experiments by rotating the tethered combination.

Above: The Apollo astronauts made one or two umbilical spacewalks on their way back from the Moon. Here Apollo 17 commander Ron Evans is hauling himself along the outside of the Apollo CSM on his way to retrieve film cassettes from the on-board external camera.

Carrying the Skylab space station, the last Saturn V launch vehicle takes to the skies from the Kennedy Space Center on 14 May 1973. Within minutes things start to go wrong. One of Skylab's solar panels is ripped off during the ascent, and another has jammed and won't deploy. The launch of the first crew of Skylab is delayed while NASA ponders what has gone wrong and what to do about it.

Below: Having earlier erected a sunshade over the damaged skin of Skylab, the astronauts are now aiming to fix the jammed solar panel. Charles Conrad (rear) is attacking the restraining strap with a pair of cable cutters. The other astronaut is Joseph Kerwin. Paul Weitz, inside Skylab's airlock module, is the photographer.

Bottom: When the first Skylab crew arrive in orbit on 25 May, they see that strapping has prevented the undamaged solar panel from deploying. For the mission to continue, the panel must be cut free, otherwise Skylab will be starved of power.

Above: Owen Garriott is picture working at the Apollo telescope mount, during the second manned Skylab mission. He has just deployed an experiment to gather interplanetary dust particles. His EVA suit is connected by umbilical to Skylab's on-board life-support system. An emergency oxygen supply is carried in the pack on the right hip.

Above left: You can gain a good idea of the size of Skylab from this still taken from a 16-mm movie film, shot during the last Skylab mission. The astronaut is solar scientist Edward Gibson.

Left: Skylab in orbit 270 miles (430 km) above the Earth in February 1974. The third Skylab crew take this picture as they prepare to return to Earth after a spectacularly successful 84-day mission. Notice the project-saving sunshade over the damaged skin of the orbital workshop. This is the second sunshade, which was put in place by two members of the second Skylab crew, Owen Garriott and Jack Lousma.

3 | Moon Walks

The dateline was 20 July 1969. The scene was the desolate Mare Tranquillitatis, or Sea of Tranquillity, one of the Moon's vast lava plains. Glinting golden in the sun, a peculiar spider-like contraption was swooping down towards the crater-marked surface. It was the Apollo 11 lunar module, code-named *Eagle.* Inside, astronaut Neil Armstrong was talking with Mission Control at Houston 240,000 miles (384,000 km) away, on planet Earth.

Houston: '60 seconds.'
Armstrong: 'Lights on. Down 2½. Forward. Forward. Good. 40 feet, down 2½. Picking up some dust. 30 feet, 2½ down. Faint shadow. 4 forward. Drifting to the right a little.'
Houston: '30 seconds.'
Armstrong: 'Drifting right. Contact light. Okay, engine stop.'
Houston: 'We copy you down, Eagle.'
Armstrong: 'Houston, Tranquillity Base here. The Eagle has landed.'
Houston: 'Roger Tranquillity, we copy you on the ground. You got a bunch of guys about to turn blue. We're breathing again. Thanks a lot.'

The Giant Leap

Inside *Eagle,* Armstrong and fellow-astronaut Buzz Aldrin, after a brief well-earned rest, donned bulky EVA suits, with their portable life-support system backpacks. Then Armstrong emerged on his hands and knees backwards out of the exit hatch, and climbed gingerly down the ladder. A few minutes later he jumped down from the last rung and planted the first human footprint on an alien world. 'That's one small step for a man,' he said, 'one giant leap for mankind.'

So began the most spectacular exploration in the history of mankind. Armstrong was soon joined by Aldrin, and together they addressed themselves first to the basic problem of moving around. Because gravity on the Moon is only one-sixth that of Earth, ordinary walking as that on Earth, is not possible. There is also the added problem that the lunar soil is full of tiny glass granules, which make it slippery.

The two pioneering lunarnauts soon adopted a bouncing, loping gait that could be likened to a kangaroo hop. For those of us back on Earth who watched the historic first moonwalk, the vision of the two ghostly-white figures bouncing over the desolate landscape, dust spurting up at each landing, looked unreal – and quite comic. It was as though we were watching an early and badly lit science-fiction movie in slow motion. One could hardly grasp that the out-of-this-world drama was actually happening, live, on our nearest neighbor in space; so near, yet so far away.

Lunar Vistas

The scene at the Apollo 11 landing site was one of 'magnificent desolation', to quote Aldrin, the lunar module pilot. The dust-covered lava plain stretched to the horizon (which is much closer than that of Earth, because the diameter of the Moon is only about one-fourth that of the Earth). The astronauts reported that the lunar soil had the consistency of newly plowed farmland on Earth. Rocks large and small protruded through it, and there were small craters all over the place, where meteorites, unhindered by an atmosphere, had showered down from space.

The astronauts, however, had precious little time to 'stand and stare'. There was much to do. They collected samples of rocks and soil and also set up equipment that would be used for experiments long after they had left. The equipment included a seismometer, used to measure moonquakes, or tremors in the Moon's crust. There was also a laser mirror, designed to reflect back a beam of laser light shot up from

On the last mission to the Moon, Apollo 17, moonwalker Eugene Cernan is about to climb into that invaluable vehicle, the lunar rover, or Moon buggy. Apollo 17 was the longest Moon mission, during which Cernan and geologist Harrison Schmitt performed three EVAs totalling over 22 hours.

telescopes on Earth. Using this apparatus scientists were later able to measure the Earth-Moon distance to an accuracy of about 6 inches! (15 cm).

After a two-and-a-half hour EVA, Armstrong and Aldrin had completed their chores and were safely back inside the lunar module, tired, covered in lunar dust, but triumphant. Ten hours later they were rocketing off the Moon to rendezvous with the parent spacecraft, the Apollo 11 CSM (command and service modules), code-named *Columbia*, which was then on its 25th orbit of the Moon. Inside, Michael Collins made the final preparations for rendezvousing and docking with the lunar module. Man's first visit to the Moon had ended.

Highlands and Lowlands

Over the next three and a half years, there were another five successful Moon-landing missions: Apollo 12, 14, 15, 16 and 17. And 10 more astronauts followed in Armstrong's and Aldrin's footsteps.

Apollo 12 made lunar landfall only four months after Apollo 11. It set down at another flat mare site on Oceanus Procellarum, the Ocean of Storms. The astronauts made a pinpoint landing less than 200 yards (180 meters) from the unmanned Surveyor 3 spacecraft, which had soft-landed there two and a half years before. As well as collecting rock and soil samples, the astronauts took back pieces of Surveyor so that scientists could gauge the effect on materials of 2½ years exposure to lunar space.

Apollo 13 (missing from the list of landings above) did set out, but was characteristically an unlucky thirteenth. When 200,000 miles (300,000 km) from Earth and closing fast with the Moon, an explosion ripped through the service module and robbed the crew module of its power and oxygen. The astronauts thankfully survived, just, by using the lunar module as a life-raft and firing its engines to push them into a free-return trajectory that took them safely back to Earth.

Apollo 14 headed towards the same landing site as Apollo 13, and this time all went well. The crew touched down near Fra Mauro crater, not far from the Apollo 12 landing site. Unlike their earlier colleagues, they had 'wheels', although just a two-wheeled handcart, which they used to carry around their tools. The Apollo 15 crew, however, had proper transport in the form of the lunar roving vehicle, nicknamed the Moon buggy. Powered by electric motors, it enabled the astronauts to venture much farther afield. Their excursions took them into the foothills of the towering Apennine Mountains and by a deep winding canyon called Hadley Rille.

Apollo 16 made a sortie into the lunar highlands, in the Cayley Plains region near the prominent Descartes crater. Apollo 17 visited Littrow Valley at the edge of Mare Serenitatis, the Sea of Serenity. One of its astronauts, geologist Jack Schmitt, was the first of a new breed of scientist-astronauts who are scientists first and astronauts second. Today, this genre of astronauts is commonplace, going into space on board the shuttle as mission and payload specialists.

By the time the 25 billion dollar Apollo Project had finished in December 1972, the 12 moonwalkers had roamed for nearly 60 miles (100 km) across the lunar surface for a total of 166 hours. They brought back with them 850 pounds (385 kg) of rocks and soil, together with more than 50 core samples from holes bored in the Moon's crust. In addition they took 30,000 photographs and collected 20,000 reels containing geophysical data. Even today, over a decade later, the analysis and interpretation of the Apollo results are not complete.

Left behind on the Moon to this day is a collection of expensive hardware totalling half a billion dollars. Beings visiting the Moon in years to come, and perhaps puzzled by what they find there, will be enlightened by the plaque attached to the Apollo 11 lunar module, which reads:

'Here men from planet Earth first set foot on the Moon, July 1969 AD. We came in peace for all mankind.'

Right: The final chapter in the Apollo lunar explorations closes on 19 December 1972, when the Apollo 17 command (crew) module splashes down in the Pacific Ocean. Here crew commander Ronald Evans is winched aboard a recovery ship helicopter. The command module, just a few meters high, is all that remains of the gigantic Saturn V rocket that had blasted off from the Kennedy Space Center 12 days and half a million miles before.

Right: Packing the power of a fleet of jumbo jets, a Saturn V Moon rocket blasts off from Complex 39 at the Kennedy Space Center in Florida in December 1968. It is carrying the Apollo 7 spacecraft with astronauts Frank Borman, James Lovell and William Anders on board. This is the first flight to the Moon, although the astronauts will go into lunar orbit and won't land. It is a vital proving flight for the 365 ft (111 meter) tall Saturn V and Apollo spacecraft systems.

Far right: En route for the Moon, the Apollo astronauts took some stunning photographs of the Earth as it receded into the distance. The Apollo 11 crew, who pioneered the Moon landings, took this shot, which shows much of the continent of Africa and the Middle East.

Above: A tired but triumphant Neil Armstrong just after he has successfully set down the fragile Apollo 11 lunar module *Eagle* on the Sea of Tranquillity on 20 July 1969. After a six-hour rest, he is to take his momentous step for mankind and set foot on another world.

Right: Edwin Aldrin steps down gingerly from the Apollo 11 lunar module's ladder to become the second man on the Moon, following in Neil Armstrong's footsteps. The landscape is barren, colorless and flat, typical of the Moon's vast *mare* regions, which are great dust-covered lava plains.

Far right: Edwin Aldrin poses for what is destined to become the most famous of all space photographs. Photographer Neil Armstrong is seen reflected in Aldrin's gold-tinted EVA visor. So is the Apollo 11 lunar module. Note how close the lunar horizon appears. This is because the Moon is so small compared with the Earth.

Above: The Apollo 11 astronauts set up a number of experiments on the lunar surface. Here Aldrin is standing by a panel erected to see how it is affected by the solar wind – a stream of particles that comes from the Sun.

Right: A wider view of the Apollo 11 landing site, snapped by Armstrong. In the foreground is some of the experimental equipment deployed by the astronauts. There is a laser reflector and (in the middle) a seismometer to measure 'moonquakes'. In the background, to the left of the lunar module, flies a specially stiffened 'Stars and Stripes'.

Below: A thin section of one of the lunar rock samples brought back to the Earth by Apollo 11. It shows in different colors a variety of fine mineral crystals. When the Moon rocks from the six different landing sites are fully investigated, it is found that the Moon has slightly different kinds of minerals from those on Earth. But it contains no new elements. Most lunar rocks are either volcanic, like basalt, or are composed of cemented rock chips, like breccia.

Below: Safely back on *terra firma,* the pioneering Apollo 11 lunarnauts are put into quarantine for a fortnight, just in case they have picked up any Moon 'bugs'. Fortunately the lunar environment is found to be sterile, and this practice is soon discontinued. Here the astronauts are sharing a joke with President Nixon, who has come to congratulate them. They are (from left to right) Neil Armstrong, Edwin Aldrin and Michael Collins.

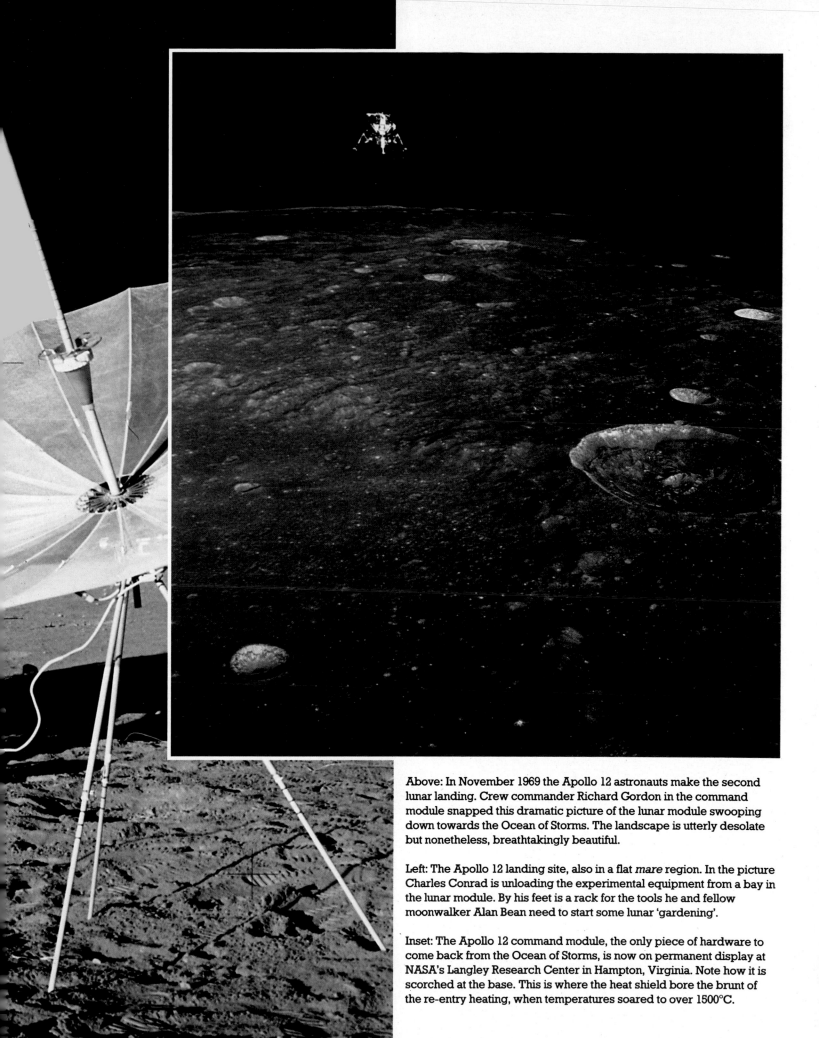

Above: In November 1969 the Apollo 12 astronauts make the second lunar landing. Crew commander Richard Gordon in the command module snapped this dramatic picture of the lunar module swooping down towards the Ocean of Storms. The landscape is utterly desolate but nonetheless, breathtakingly beautiful.

Left: The Apollo 12 landing site, also in a flat *mare* region. In the picture Charles Conrad is unloading the experimental equipment from a bay in the lunar module. By his feet is a rack for the tools he and fellow moonwalker Alan Bean need to start some lunar 'gardening'.

Inset: The Apollo 12 command module, the only piece of hardware to come back from the Ocean of Storms, is now on permanent display at NASA's Langley Research Center in Hampton, Virginia. Note how it is scorched at the base. This is where the heat shield bore the brunt of the re-entry heating, when temperatures soared to over 1500°C.

Above: Apparatus set up by the Apollo 14 astronauts as part of the automatic ALSEP (Apollo lunar surface experiments package) scientific station. In the foreground is the power module, or RTG (radioisotope thermoelectric generator). The Apollo 14 EVAs took place in the lunar uplands near Fra Mauro crater on 5 and 6 February 1971.

Right: This is part of the makeshift life-support apparatus that the Apollo 13 astronauts rigged up after an explosion crippled their craft 200,000 miles (300,000 km) from Earth. In this picture, taken in the lunar module liferaft, the astronaut is John Swigert.

Above: Technicians at the Kennedy Space Center preparing the Apollo 15 lunar module for the fourth lunar landing mission. They are stowing the collapsible lunar roving vehicle, or Moon buggy. This battery-powered Moon jeep was developed at a cost of some $15 million.

Next page: One of the finest Apollo surface photographs taken during the Apollo 15 mission in July/August 1971. Astronaut James Irwin salutes the 'Stars and Stripes', planted in the lunar dust at the foot of the Apennine mountain range on the edge of Mare Imbrium, the Sea of Showers. He and fellow moonwalker David Scott have just unpacked the lunar rover, making its début on this mission. Thanks to the rover, the astronauts were able to travel much farther afield than their earlier colleagues.

Above: During the Apollo 16 mission, Charles Duke is seen working near the 130 ft (40 meter) wide Plum crater. He is boring into the ground for a core sample. Study of the various layers in the core samples gives lunar scientists clues to the history of the Moon. Notice the lunar rover parked on the far side of the crater.

Left: Tire marks and footprints in the lunar dust in the Descartes highlands during the Apollo 16 EVA. The astronaut is Charles Duke. The instrument in the foreground is a gnomon. It is a device used for calibrating pictures of the surface. It provides a vertical rod of known length and a color chart.

Far left: Seconds after lift-off on 16 April 1972, Apollo 16 climbs from the launch pad on a pillar of smoke and flame. In less than a quarter of an hour the spacecraft, with third stage still attached, will be in orbit, circling the Earth at 17,500 mph (28,000 km/h). Later the third stage will fire again and blast the spacecraft into a trans-lunar trajectory.

43

Top left: One of the 'classic' Apollo photographs, showing Apollo 17 geologist Harrison Schmitt with the US flag and, a quarter of a million miles away, the Earth. The flag and photographer Eugene Cernan can be seen reflected in Schmitt's visor.

Left: On the final Apollo mission (17) geologist-astronaut Harrison Schmitt gets down to some lunar 'gardening' with his custom-built rake. Actually he is using the rake to collect rock chips of a certain size. In the background are the rolling Taurus mountains.

Above: Eugene Cernan test drives the Apollo 17 lunar rover before loading it with equipment. The collapsible rover is made of lightweight aluminum tubing and wire. About 10 ft (3 meters) long, it has a width of 6 ft (1.8 meters). It is driven by battery-powered electric motors on each wheel. In this 'stripped-down' state it is capable of a maximum speed of nearly 10 mph (16 km/h).

4 | Shuttlewalks

In February 1984 on space shuttle mission 41-B, the orbiter *Challenger* soared into the Florida skies with an ambitious flight schedule ahead. It was to launch two communications satellites, *Westar VI* and *Palapa B-2* (for Indonesia); flight test the manned maneuvering unit (MMU) for the first time; rehearse procedures for recovering a dead satellite; and make the first landing at the Kennedy launch site.

After the 8-day mission NASA could report good news and bad news. One piece of good news was that the MMU worked perfectly, leading to Bruce McCandless becoming the world's first astronaut to make an untethered spacewalk. The second piece of good news was that *Challenger* made a successful landing at the Kennedy Space Center.

The bad news, however, was really bad. Both of the satellites launched from the orbiter had malfunctioned and were in low orbits. It was particularly bad news for the satellite insurers, because they stood to lose no less than $180 million! Nine months later, however, these same insurers were grinning broadly. Shuttle astronauts, with some spectacular feats of spacewalking, had plucked both the errant satellites from orbit and returned them to Earth. After a quick checkover they would be as good as new and ready for sale to the highest bidder. With astounding success, the era of satellite recovery had begun.

The Shuttle Spacesuit
The shuttle astronauts do not need to wear spacesuits when they fly into orbit. Their crew cabin is fully pressurized, just like an airliner is on Earth. Only when they leave the orbiting shuttle do they put on spacesuits, which are correctly termed EMUs, or extravehicular mobility units. The shuttle suit is a development of the Apollo suit, successfully used by the Apollo and Skylab astronauts. It is made up of many layers, which apply pressure to the body and protect it from external temperature extremes and radiation.

Unlike the Apollo suit, however, the shuttle suit is made in two pieces – an upper torso and trousers. The upper torso is a rigid structure with a frame of aluminum. It connects with a metal waist ring at the top of the otherwise flexible trousers. The upper torso has a portable life-support system built in. All the connections between it and the suit are made internally, so there are no external hoses and connections as there were on the Apollo suit.

Beneath the suit, the astronaut puts on water-cooled long johns, which keep his body cool. He also wears a urine collecting device. One other feature of the long johns is a drink's bag, from which the astronaut can sip water during the EVA.

On board the shuttle orbiter, the two-piece spacesuit is stored inside the airlock, which is a cylindrical chamber located at the rear of the mid-deck. The astronauts enter through a hatch from the mid-deck. When they are suited up, typically only a 5-minute operation, they depressurize the airlock and open a hatch leading into the orbiter's payload bay.

The astronauts cannot, however, get suited up immediately they enter the airlock. First they have to breathe a pure oxygen atmosphere for at least two hours. This is to flush out nitrogen dissolved in the blood. If the nitrogen were allowed to remain, it would bubble out of the blood when the astronauts put on their suits, which operate at low pressure. They would then get a severe and crippling attack of 'the bends'.

The MMU
The shuttle manned maneuvering unit (MMU) evolved from a model that was first tested inside the cavernous Skylab space station. It is a

Having successfully completed the recovery of the *Palapa B-2* and *Westar VI* satellites in November 1984, Dale Gardner begins the first in-orbit advertizing campaign! Fellow helpmate and entrepreneur Joe Allen is seen reflected in Gardner's helmet visor. Allen is standing on the mobile foot restraint on the arm of the remote manipulator system.

Shuttle orbiter *Challenger*, second of the four-orbiter fleet to become operational, blasts off the launch pad of Complex 39 at the Kennedy Space Center in Florida. It first flew in space on 4 April 1983, just two years after orbiter Columbia made its maiden flight. The orbiters can carry enormous payloads totalling up to nearly 29 tons (30 tonnes) in weight. Several satellites can be accommodated at once in their cavernous cargo bay, which measures some 60 ft (18 meters) long and 15 ft (4.5 meters) across.

self-contained, jet-propelled backpack, which astronauts use to fly untethered in space. Since Bruce McCandless made the first test flight in February 1984, the MMU has proved invaluable for satellite repair (of *Solar Max* in April 1984) and recovery (of *Westar VI* and *Palapa B-2* in November 1984).

The MMU looks vaguely like an armchair, with armrests but no seat. Dotted around the outside of the unit are 24 thruster nozzles, which eject jets of nitrogen gas. The astronaut fires combinations of these thrusters to propel him in whatever direction he chooses. He controls the firing by means of two control handles on the arms. The left hand controller governs movement fore and aft, side to side and up and down. The right-hand controller handles rolling, pitching and yawing movements.

The nitrogen supply for the thrusters comes from two pressurized tanks in the rear of the MMU. These contain enough gas to support a 6-hour EVA. The nitrogen tanks can be recharged at the flight support station (FSS) at the front of the orbiter payload bay, where the MMU is stored during a mission. The FSS also has the facility to recharge the MMU's two silver-zinc batteries. These power the unit's controls and instrumentation and also three winking locator lights.

The Space Crane

Spacewalking shuttle astronauts would find life very much more difficult without the assistance of the orbiter's versatile crane, properly called the remote manipulator system (RMS) arm. It is mounted at the front of the payload bay on the left-hand side looking for'ard. It is 50 ft (15 meters) long, and has three flexible joints: a 'shoulder', where it is attached to the orbiter; an 'elbow' and a 'wrist'. At the end is a device called the end effector, which uses wire snares to grip things.

Two of the RMS's main functions are to launch satellites from the payload bay, and to retrieve satellites from orbit. Satellites designed for launch and retrieval in this way have a docking target, or grapple pin attached. When assisting the astronauts, a device called a manipulator foot restraint is attached to the end of the RMS. This is a

Below: Although the orbiter takes off like a rocket, it lands like an airplane, or rather a glider because the descent is unpowered. Here orbiter *Discovery* is on the point of making a perfect touchdown at Edwards Air Force Base in California. Edwards AFB is one of the alternative landing sites for the shuttle if the runway at the Kennedy Space Center becomes non-operational because of adverse weather conditions.

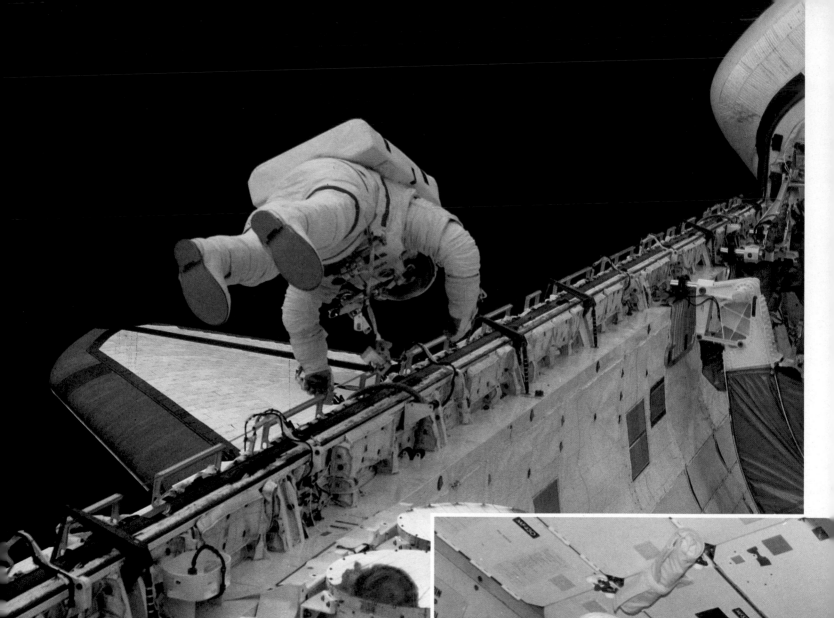

platform with straps, that secure the astronaut's feet and prevent him floating away when working. It is often called a 'cherry picker' because it is like the hydraulic-lift platform used for picking cherries, mending telephone lines, and so on.

The Stinger

For the capture of the *Palapa* and *Westar* satellites mentioned earlier, another item of hardware was required. These satellites were not fitted with a grapple pin and so could not be gripped by the RMS arm. Astronaut Dale Gardner, who was to be involved in the capture mission, came up with an alternative idea, which he sketched on the back of an envelope. It was a spear-like probe that would fit into the propulsion motor nozzle of the satellites and lock. The 'stinger' was born. NASA, of course, came up with an exceedingly long name for it – the Apogee Kick Motor Capture Device (ACD).

During the capture mission, the shuttle orbiter chased each satellite and maneuvered to within about 35 ft (11 meters). Flying an MMU and riding the stinger, the astronaut jetted over to the spinning satellite. He then inserted the stinger and locked onto the motor nozzle. With bursts of his MMU jets, he stopped the satellite spinning and then jetted back to the waiting orbiter. There, the RMS arm reached out and grasped a grapple pin on the stinger to capture the satellite. The satellite was then lowered into the payload bay. But the final stowing of the satellite had to be done by hand, proving once again the need for the human touch in space maneuvers.

Left, main picture: Story Musgrave pulls himself along the hand rails on the edge of *Challenger's* payload bay. He is checking out the new shuttle spacesuit for the first time in orbit on shuttle mission STS-6 in April 1983. For safety he is tethered to a safety wire, which runs all the way along the bay. Shuttle suits were supposed to have been tested on an earlier mission, but the tests were cancelled when the suits malfunctioned, fortunately in the airlock prior to EVA.

Bottom left, inset: Seen here during mission 41-G, in October 1984, Kathryn Sullivan and fellow spacewalker David Leestma are trying to catch their helmets while making preparations for EVA. Part of a shuttle suit can be seen on the right.

Above: Here Story Musgrave (left) has been joined by Donald Peterson on the STS-6 mission. They are pictured at the aft end of the payload bay making a tethered spacewalk as they speed over Mexico at nearly 17,500 mph (28,000 km/h).

Top right, inset: Kathryn Sullivan making her historic spacewalk on 11 October 1984. Note the tether line on the right. She is checking the latch of the shuttle imaging radar antenna, which is causing problems on the mission by refusing to deploy. But Dr Sullivan's main task on EVA is to take part in a simulation with David Leestma, of in-orbit spacecraft refuelling.

Above: The shuttle RMS arm under test at Spar Aerospace in Toronto, Canada. It is 50 ft (15 meters) long and is so heavy on Earth that it must be supported. It works perfectly, however, under zero-G conditions in orbit. The picture gives some idea of the complex construction of the arm joints. In space, the arm is blanketed with white insulation.

Far left: A superb view of orbiter *Challenger,* snapped against a cloud-flecked atmosphere during the STS-7 mission. It was taken by a camera aboard the shuttle payload pallet (SPAS). It shows on the port side the location of the shuttle crane, the Canadian-built remote manipulator system (RMS) arm, which was used to launch SPAS into space. At the rear of the payload bay are protective cradles for Palapa and Telesat communications satellites.

Left: The control console of the RMS simulator at Spar Aerospace. It is a mock-up of the aft flight deck of the orbiter, from where mission specialist astronauts control the RMS in real time. Above the console is the translational hand controller, which moves the arm up and down or from side to side. Below right is the rotational hand controller for rotating the arm. The two screens on the right are linked on the real arm to TV cameras on the 'elbow' and end effector.

Left: The RMS arm being used in February 1984 for a somewhat different purpose, to carry a mobile foot restraint, popularly called a 'cherry picker'. Hitching a ride on the cherry picker is Bruce McCandless, shortly to become the first astronaut to make an untethered spacewalk.

Above: *Challenger's* RMS arm launches the gold-foil covered Earth radiation budget satellite (ERBS) in October 1984. It is gripping by its end effector, which has snared a grapple pin on the satellite. Note the closed-circuit TV camera mounted on top of the end effector.

Right: Astronauts in the forward end of the shuttle orbiter, by the crew compartment bulkhead. The circular open hatch in the bulkhead leads into the airlock, where the astronauts get kitted up. The astronauts are Bruce McCandless (left) and Robert Stewart. McCandless is standing at the port side flight support station in which the manned maneuvering unit (MMU) is stored. Note the two windows at the top of the bulkhead. They allow astronauts on the orbiter flight deck to look out into the payload bay.

Below: Bruce McCandless makes the first untethered spacewalk on 7 February 1984, becoming a human satellite. He is flying the MMU, the 'Buck-Rogers' style jet-propelled backpack. With controlled bursts of its 24 thrusters, he will eventually jet away to a maximum distance of some 300 ft (90 meters) before returning.

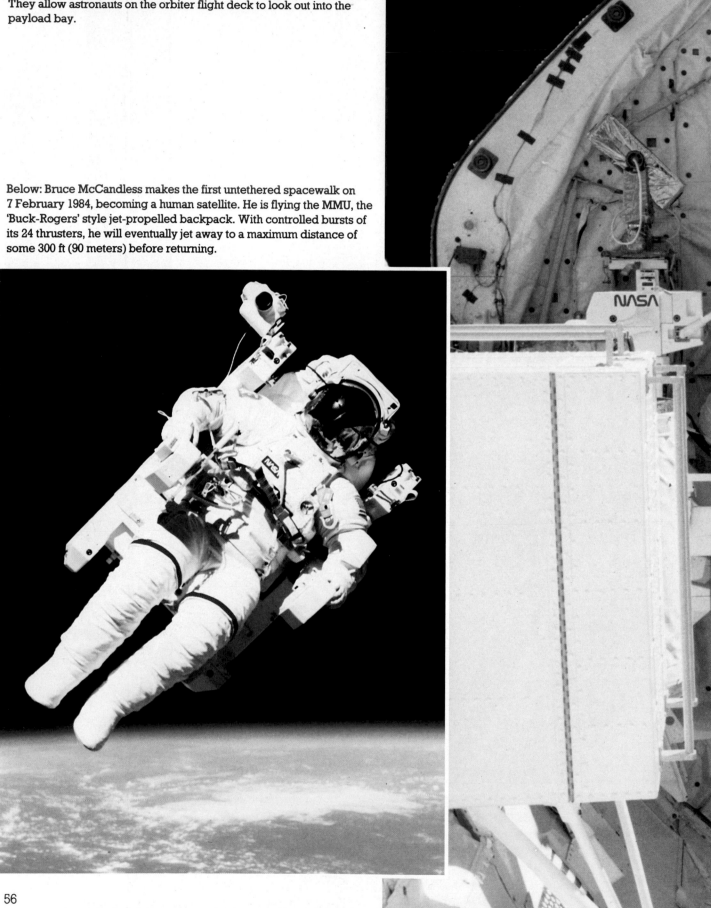

Main picture: The solar maximum mission satellite (*Solar Max*), target for the 41-C shuttle mission in April 1984. *Solar Max* was the first satellite designed for retrieval by the shuttle for servicing or repair. Launched in 1980, it worked for only 8 months before its attitude-control system failed. Since then it had been tumbling out of control and was, for all intents and purposes, useless.

Top right: The objective of the 41-C mission was for astronaut George Nelson to jet over to *Solar Max* in an MMU. He would then dock with it using a purpose-built docking device. Next he would stabilize the tumbling satellite and jet back with it to the orbiter. Here he is seen rendezvousing with *Solar Max*. But despite every effort, he is unable to dock with it.

Bottom right: Eventually *Solar Max* is captured using the RMS arm and, with the help of astronauts George Nelson and James Van Hoften, is stored in the payload bay. Here, Nelson is carried on a tour of inspection around *Solar Max* on the RMS 'cherry picker'. Note the TV camera mounted on the RMS's 'elbow'. Nelson and Van Hoften successfully mend the satellite, and it is re-launched into orbit, working perfectly.

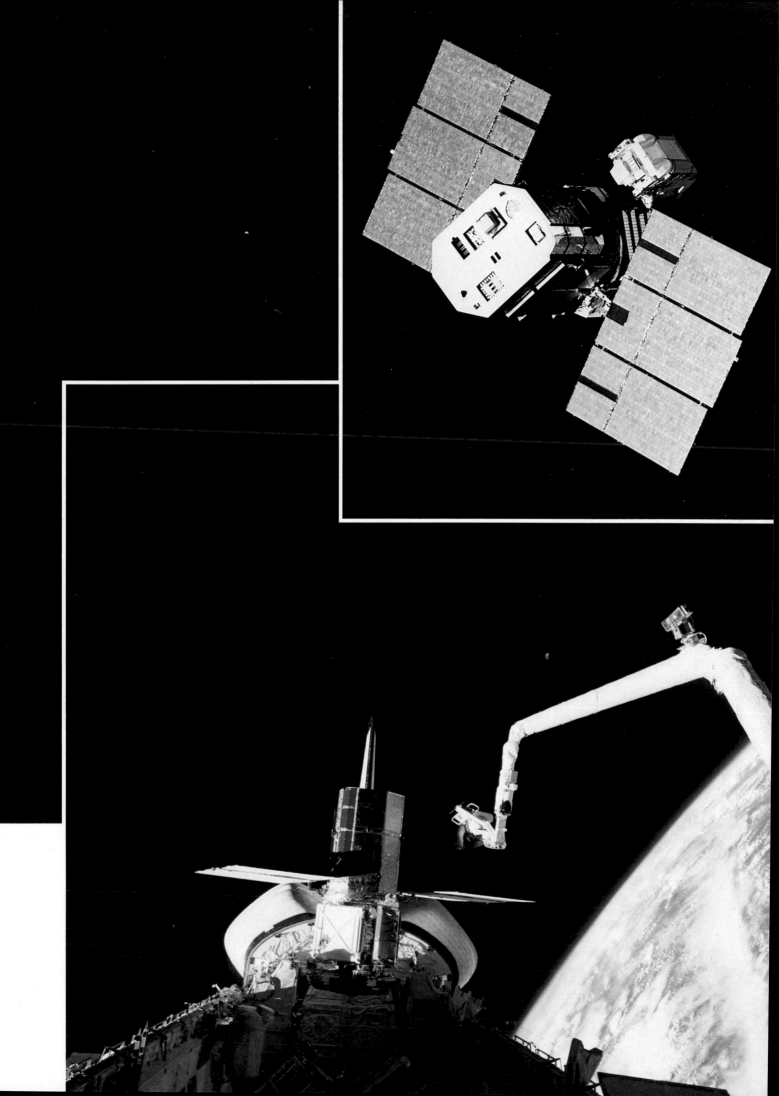

Above: Dale Gardner rides the stinger this time to mate with the *Westar VI* satellite. He will then fire the jets of his MMU to stop the satellite spinning and then jet back with it to the waiting orbiter, where his partner is waiting on the 'cherry picker' at the end of the RMS arm.

Main picture: Capture of the huge *Palapa B-2,* the first of two rogue communications satellites, which astronauts recovered from orbit on mission 51-A in November 1984. Astronaut Joe Allen (left) and Dale Gardner are about to secure the satellite in the payload bay. The 'stinger' Allen used to mate with the satellite before bringing it back is seen at bottom right.

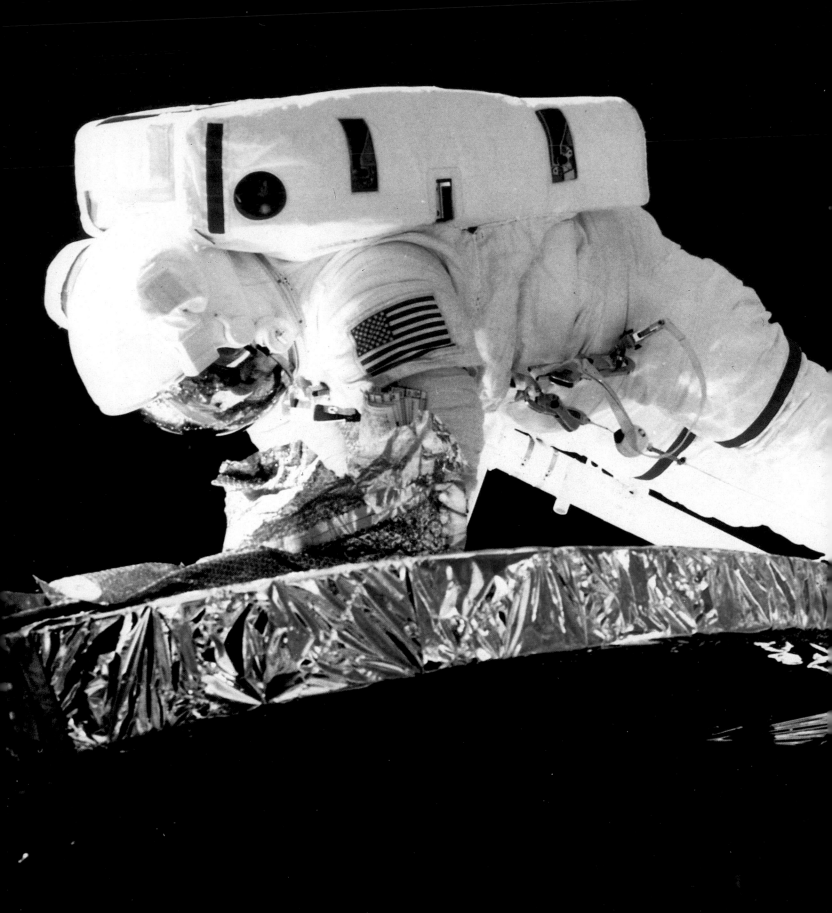

Inset below: Perched triumphantly above the satellites they have captured, Gardner (with the 'For Sale' notice) and Allen pause to clown for a while before returning into the orbiter. Back in London, England, Lloyds insurance underwriters, which had been the major insurers of the two satellites, rang the famous Lutine Bell twice. This is traditional when a particularly successful salvage operation takes place.

Main picture, left: His feet anchored to the 'cherry picker', Joe Allen gently nudges the *Westar VI* satellite into the orbiter's cargo bay near the completion of the satellite recovery operations, on mission 51-A. Out of sight beneath the satellite is fellow spacewalker Dale Gardner. Operating the RMS arm from inside the orbiter is Anna Fisher.

Above: With a job well done, the crew of the 51-A recovery mission pose for a group portrait. '2 up' refers to two satellites launched. '2 down' refers to 2 satellites recovered. The crew are, from left to right: back row, Dale Gardner and Frederick Hauck; front row, David Walker, Anna Fisher and Joe Allen.

5 | Space Spidermen

The space shuttle orbiter is currently the largest body to be found in space. Some 122 ft (37 meters) from nose to tail, it is more than 25 ft (8 meters) longer than the Soviet space station Salyut when its Soyuz ferry craft are docked with it. But NASA planners are looking forward to the days when the orbiter will be shuttling up to visit structures tens and even hundreds of times its size.

The biggest ones would be solar power satellites (SPS), which would beam solar energy captured in orbit down to the Earth in the form of microwaves. They could provide part of the solution to the 21st century's energy problems. To produce sufficient power, say 5000 megawatts, they would need to be roughly 6 miles (10 km) long and 3 miles (5 km) across. Weighing 19,500 tons (20,000 tonnes), their construction would require a labor force of about 500 workers for perhaps a year.

Ambitious projects like the SPS, however, are very much in the future. The present plans for expanding the human presence in space are much more modest. They call for the establishment of a permanent space station in the 1990s, relatively small at first but capable of progressive expansion into a large complex. For many years NASA research centers and private companies like Boeing and Rockwell have carried out preliminary planning in space station design and construction. But not until January 1984 was NASA given the official go-ahead to develop a space-station program. A budget of 8 billion dollars was allocated.

The Modular Approach

The first successful American space station, Skylab, was a one-off design. It was put together using hardware left over from the Apollo Project. And it was launched, fully assembled in one piece, by a spare Saturn V Moon rocket. The '90s space station, however, will be constructed of modules that will be delivered separately into orbit by the shuttle and then assembled there *in situ.*

Spacewalking shuttle astronauts will play a key role in constructing the station. They will use similar techniques to the ones they used in capturing and securing the rogue communications satellites in November 1984. They will don their jet-propelled backpacks, or manned maneuvering units (MMUs), and manhandle the modules into position for docking with connecting structures. They will work in conjunction with the shuttle orbiter's remote manipulator system (RMS) arm, which will be manned by one of the mission specialists from inside the orbiter.

The initial space station would probably be made up of three modules linked to a tubular connecting structure, also modular in construction. This would have spare docking ports to allow the addition of extra modules and periodic visits by a service shuttle. It would also probably house the main life-support system, communications and control centers, and station power system. Power would be provided by large arrays of solar cells located on long booms.

One of the main modules would be fitted out as a habitat, or living module. It would include separate living quarters for each crew member (sheer luxury after the share-and-share-alike shuttle orbiter facilities), a recreation room, bathroom and galley (kitchen). A second module would be equipped as a scientific laboratory (rather like the present Spacelab flown in the shuttle). A third would be a logistics, or re-supply module. This would act as a storeroom for supplies and materials, such as food, water and rocket propellants. When supplies have run down, a shuttle would bring up another re-filled unit from Earth and take the empty one back.

Some time next century, high-flying spidermen will get to grips with gigantic space structures like this solar power station. The scale of such an enterprise is formidable. The solar collectors will need to be several miles across. Periodically, shuttle craft will visit the construction base, bringing fresh crews and supplies. Raw materials and heavy equipment will be carried into orbit by heavy-lift launch vehicles like the one on the left of the picture.

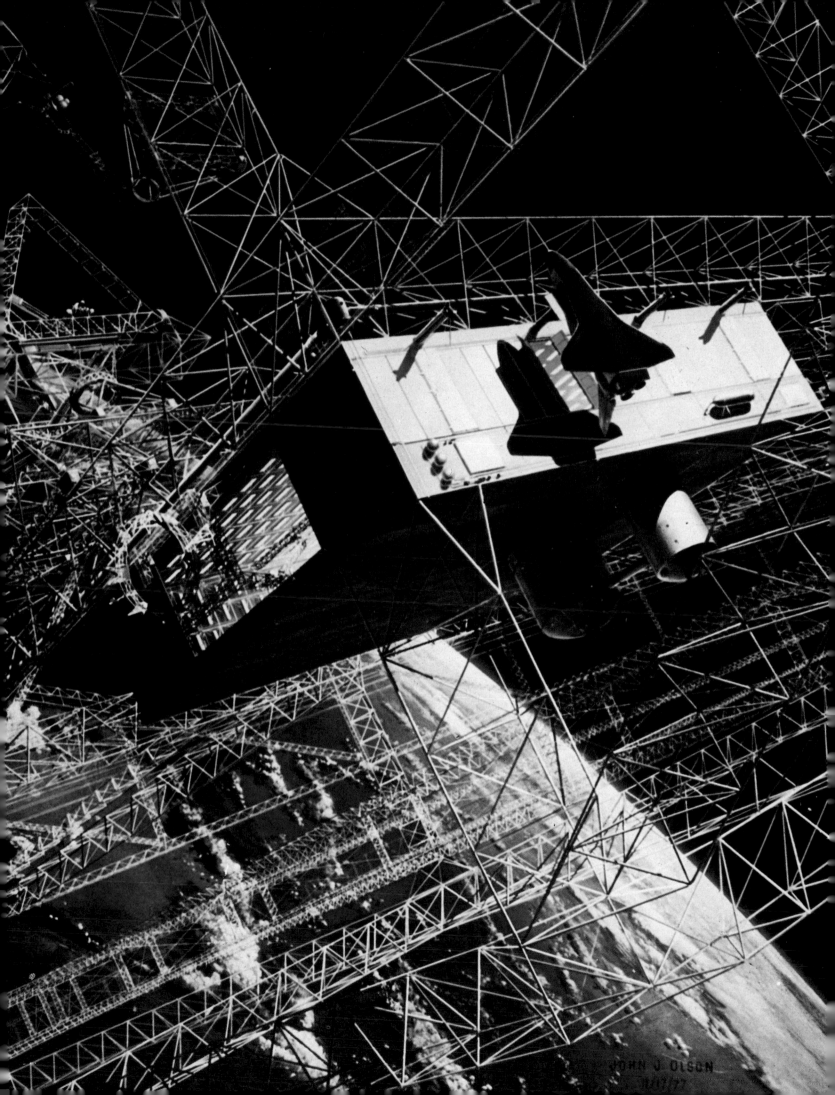

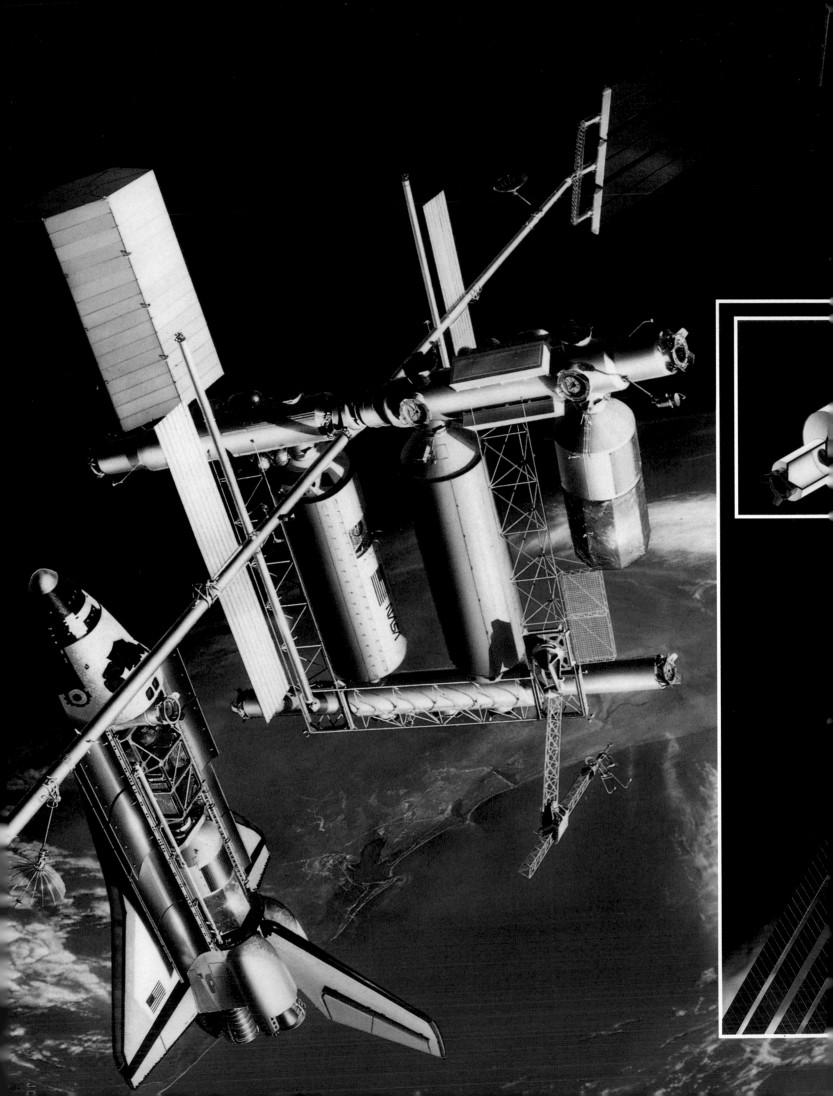

Expansion

Once the basic space station has become established and its performance verified, it will be quickly expanded, with a larger crew and new laboratories. The crew will take over from the shuttle the role of satellite service, recovery and repair. They will also become more involved with other space construction projects.

One of the first will be the construction of free-flying platforms. These will be designed to carry a number of independent scientific experiments, from different researchers. The various pieces of apparatus will operate separately, but will utilize the power, communications and attitude-control systems of the platform. This makes much better economic sense than each experiment having independent systems.

To begin with, the space platforms will be built by fitting together trussed beams ferried up in the shuttle orbiter's payload bay. The astronauts, jetting about in their MMUs, will manually maneuver the beams into position with the help of the RMS arm and lock them together with a suitable fastener.

Recent tests by Langley Research Center scientists, however, have suggested that this method of construction would be too fatiguing. So they have developed a machine called the Swing-Arm Beam Erector (SABER), which is a kind of mobile work platform. The astronaut stands on the platform, which can move around the axis of the structure under construction on a swing arm, and also along the axis on a telescopic arm. Langley scientists have tested this machine very successfully in the simulated weightless conditions of Marshall Space Flight Center's water tank, or neutral buoyancy chamber.

The next step beyond erecting ready-made beams is actually to manufacture beams on the spot, in orbit. For large structures this would save scores of trips from Earth by shuttle, which could only carry a few lengths of the ready-made beams at a time. With *in situ* fabrication in mind, Grumman Aerospace have already designed a prototype beam builder. And it works. It takes narrow spools of sheet aluminum, and heats, shapes and welds them into a rigid trussed beam of triangular cross-section. A single shuttle orbiter could carry enough spools to build a beam thousands of yards long.

On the Move

At present, when a shuttle crew set out to recover a satellite, they first have to maneuver so as to match its orbit. The space station will not be able to do this. The crew will therefore require an in-orbit shuttle craft to enable them to rendezvous with satellites that need servicing. Designs for such an orbital maneuvering vehicle are already underway.

The vehicle would probably only be used initially for rendezvousing with low-orbiting craft. High-flying satellites in 'stationary' orbit some 22,300 miles (36,000 km) high will probably be retrieved by robot tugs controlled remotely by the station crew. It is dangerous for human beings to fly so high because they will be subjected to the intense radiation of the Van Allen belts.

Later robots will be much more versatile. They will be designed to repair satellites on the spot, without the need to bring them back to the space station service center. The robot satellite repairer, or teleoperator, would have mechanical hands and arms (probably three), which would be equally as dextrous as the human hand and arm. It would have stereo television cameras as eyes. And it would be controlled remotely from the space station by a human operator with special sensors attached to his body. Whatever the human operator did, the robot would imitate. It would become an extension of the human operator's senses and muscles.

In time such robots will almost certainly replace spacewalking astronauts for routine EVA duties. This will be all to the good. As major space construction projects get underway in the next decade, more and more astronauts will be required to risk their lives, and go EVA. Accidents are bound to happen as they do on every construction project. In space, however, there is virtually no margin for error. A snag in the spacesuit or a blocked valve in the oxygen supply would mean instant disaster.

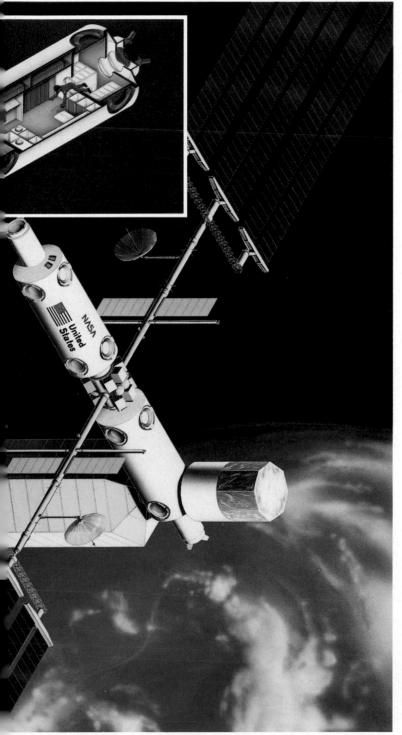

Left: A relatively simple space station design of the type that could be in orbit by the end of the century. It is made up of two main habitat modules, which have docking ports at both ends and on the sides. Large solar arrays provide electricity to power the station. At top right is a logistics module, which holds supplies for the station. It is replaced by shuttle every few months. At lower right is a hanger, which protects orbital vehicles and visiting Earth craft from space debris.

Inset left: A look inside a typical space station module, which is double-skinned for safety. Various kinds of equipment may be installed, depending on the module's function.

Main picture, far left: Here the space station has been considerably expanded by the addition of extra modules. The shuttle is paying one of its periodic visits to re-supply the station with provisions, mail and propellants. They are carried in the logistics module in the cargo bay.

Left: A busy scene in Earth orbit as construction proceeds on a solar power station. (Note the scale of the operation from the size of the attendant shuttle craft.) Several beam-building machines are at work. Some of the free-flying units are remote-controlled robots, worked by astronaut engineers at the construction control center. Others are pressurized work stations containing human operators. They are equipped with mechanical arms, as versatile as human limbs, but infinitely stronger.

Inset left: This is a prototype beam builder developed for NASA by Grumman Aerospace. It takes rolls of aluminum sheet (on top and bottom) and bends, cuts and welds them into a continuous beam. The beam, of triangular cross-section, can be seen emerging from the machine on the left of the picture.

Below: Large space structures such as communications platforms and power satellites will be built using simple trussed aluminum beams. These will be fabricated in orbit by machines called beam builders. The machines will be operated initially from inside the orbiter's cargo bay, as shown in the picture. Astronauts will be on hand to oversee the operation and help join the beams together.

Above: Come next century, construction could begin on vast space city-colonies, in which thousands of people will live and work. Here, work is almost finished on a torus, or wheel-shaped colony. The people will be housed in the tube, in which an artificial Earth landscape will be created. The tube measures about 500 ft (150 meters) across. The whole wheel structure has a diameter of over a mile. It will be rotated to create an artificial gravity. 'Up' will be towards the hub of the wheel.

Right: In this alternative space colony design a population of about 10,000 people live in the central sphere, which is rotated to create artificial gravity. Light is reflected inside by saucer-shaped mirrors adjacent to the sphere, which receive sunlight from the ring of mirrors girdling the center of the sphere. The two sets of rings, or toruses, in this design, are set aside for agricultural use. The large panels at each end of the complex are radiators for ridding the colony of excess heat.